Date: 8/1/18

J 621.811 RUS
Rustad, Martha E. H.
Levers /

Simple Machines

Levers

by Martha E. H. Rustad

CAPSTONE PRESS
a capstone imprint

Little Pebble is published by Capstone Press,
1710 Roe Crest Drive, North Mankato, Minnesota 56003
www.mycapstone.com

Library of Congress Cataloging-in-Publication Data
Names: Rustad, Martha E. H. (Martha Elizabeth Hillman), 1975– author.
Title: Levers / by Martha E.H. Rustad.
Description: North Mankato, Minnesota : Capstone Press, 2018. | Series:
    Little pebble. Simple machines | Audience: Ages 4-7.
Identifiers: LCCN 2017031579 (print) | LCCN 2017042207 (ebook) |
    ISBN 9781543500875 (eBook PDF) | ISBN 9781543500752 (hardcover) |
    ISBN 9781543500813 (paperback)
Subjects: LCSH: Levers—Juvenile literature.
Classification: LCC TJ147 (ebook) | LCC TJ147 .R88 2018 (print) | DDC
    621.8—dc23
LC record available at https://lccn.loc.gov/2017031579

Editorial Credits

Marissa Kirkman, editor; Kyle Grentz (cover) and Charmaine Whitman (interior), designers; Jo Miller, media researcher; Katy LaVigne, production specialist

Image Credits

Capstone Studio: Karon Dubke, 19; iStockphoto: asiseeit, 13, Image Source, 5, kall9, 11, stigmatize, 15; Shutterstock: 3445128471, 20, Andris Tkacenko, 17 (bottom), Anneka, 24, Kristina Postnikova, cover, 1, Shcherbakov Ilya, 7, Syda Productions, 17 (top), Volcko Mar, 9, wavebreakmedia, 21

Design Elements
Capstone

Printed and bound in the USA.
010766S18

Table of Contents

Levers Help

Work is hard!

We need help.

Use a simple machine.

These tools help us work.

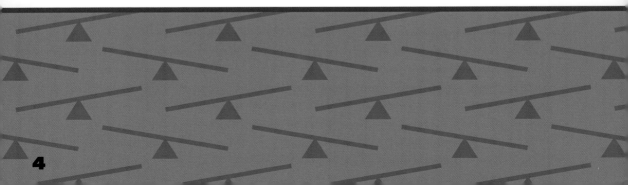

lever

A lever helps us lift.

A lever helps move loads.

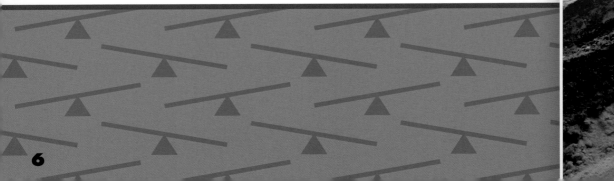

lever

How Levers Work

A lever is a bar.

It sits on a point.

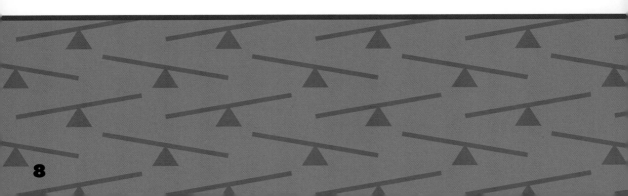

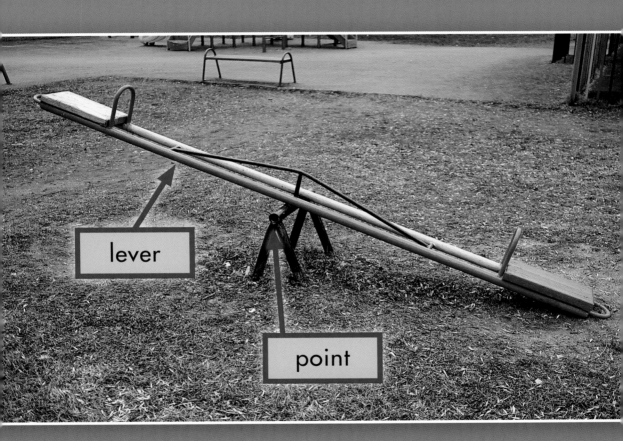

lever

point

Push down on a lever.

The other side moves up.

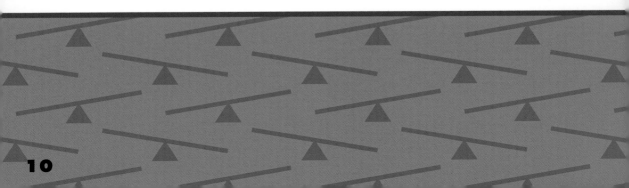

lever

Put a big load on

one end of the lever.

Push down.

Lift the load!

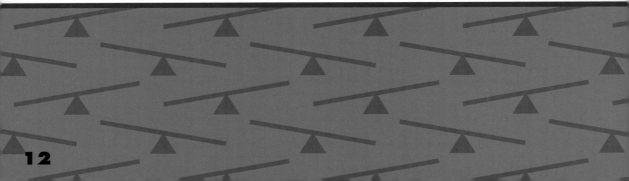

lever

load

Everyday Levers

A seesaw is a lever.

Push!

A friend goes up.

You go down.

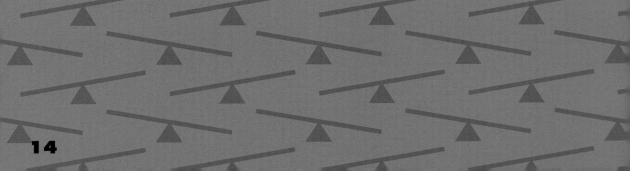

A hammer is a lever.

Pull!

A nail comes out.

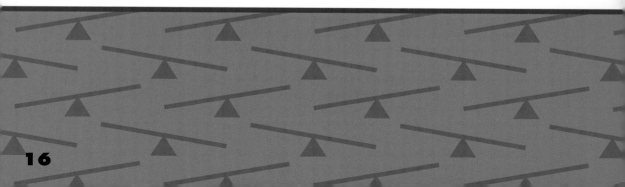

Scissors are levers.

Squeeze!

The paper is cut.

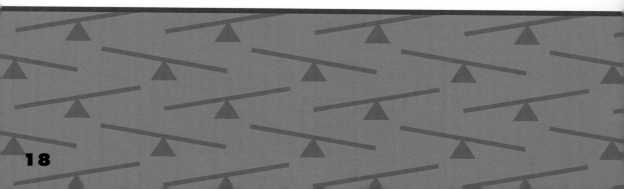

We use a simple machine.

It makes work easier and fun.

lever

Glossary

bar—a long, stiff stick or flat block

lever—a bar that you can use to lift a load by putting one end under the load and pushing down on the other end; a lever is a simple machine

load—an object that you want to move or lift

point—the end or tip of an object; a lever turns on a point called a fulcrum

scissors—a tool used to cut paper; scissors are two levers stuck together

simple machine—a tool that makes it easier to move something

work—a job that must be done

Read More

Miller, Tim and Rebecca Sjonger. *Levers in My Makerspace.* Simple Machines in My Makerspace. New York: Crabtree Publishing, 2017.

Rivera, Andrea. *Levers.* Simple Machines. Minneapolis: Abdo Zoom, 2017.

Weakland, Mark. *Fred Flintstone's Adventures with Levers: Lift that Load!* Flintstones Explain Simple Machines. North Mankato, Minn.: Capstone Press, 2016.

Internet Sites

Use FactHound to find Internet sites related to this book.

Visit www.facthound.com

Just type in 9781543500752 and go.

Super-cool stuff! Check out projects, games and lots more at **www.capstonekids.com**

Critical Thinking Questions

1. What does a lever sit on?

2. What happens when you push down on one side of a lever?

3. Have you ever used a lever? How did it help you?

Index